Kids on the Inside Looking Out After Loss

William Steele, M.A., M.S.W.

KIDSRIGHTS®

KIDS ON THE INSIDE
LOOKING OUT AFTER LOSS

Published by:
KIDSRIGHTS®
10100 Park Cedar Drive
Charlotte, NC 28210
800/892-5437 or 704/541-0100

10 9 8 7 6 5 4 3 2

Second Printing

Printed in the United States of America.

ISBN: 1-55864-036-3

ACKNOWLEDGEMENTS

In 1993 The Community Foundation for Southeastern Michigan supported the Trauma Referral Network Project. The project's participants assessed 200 children 3-16 years of age and provided them intervention for posttraumatic stress disorder. The children's traumatic experiences and the counselors' positive responses to both the process and the results compelled us to publish *KIDS*.

We want to give special thanks to the Trauma Referral Network Project participants; many continue to work with us. Their willingness and commitment to bring long needed resources to others who work with traumatized children made KIDS possible.

TRAUMA REFERRAL NETWORK PARTICIPANTS

Tina Bersano	Bay County
Carolyn Grawi-Brandt	Washtenaw County
Ilene Cohen	Oakland County
Barry Eitel	Monroe County
Karen L. Hunt	Wayne County
Jo Lynne Juengel	Macomb County
Patrina Pica-Kras	Macomb County
Mark Maxim	Monroe County
Barbara McCarthy	Macomb County
Marie Moreland	Shiawassee County
Linda Pallos	Wayne County
Douglas F. Roby	Wayne County
Berry Schumer	Monroe County
Cora Schlieman Taylor	Wayne County

Our very special thank you to Parents of Murdered Children, Metro Detroit Chapter, a support group for all survivors of homicide. Several children from this organization courageously shared their trauma experience. Their stories and their dramatic drawings are at the heart of *KIDS.*

Thank you to Melvyn Raider, Associate Professor, Wayne State University School of Social Work for his evaluation and assessment of traumatized children for an earlier project.

TLC staff also acknowledges the invaluable support of New Center Community Mental Health Services, Children's Services Unit and its Executive Director, Roberta V. Sanders. Her concern for the special needs of traumatized children is long standing as she has shown through her support for this and many other projects.

Our grateful appreciation to Sue Sells whose suggestions, encouragement, and editing helped to make KIDS a useful resource.

PREFACE

KIDS: ON THE INSIDE LOOKING OUT AFTER LOSS dramatically depicts through children's drawings the images and fantasies they experience after a trauma. These images reflect the chaos, panic, and terror that parents and professionals must learn to recognize and respond to as no child can develop normally when they're haunted by terror. The children tell their stories, and discuss how their lives have suffered, how they are experiencing what we would have expected only adult survivors of war to experience.

Their cry is more than a cry for help; it is the sound of terror, the scream in the night that can find no voice. *KIDS* helps us to recognize their silent terror and how to help them find relief.

KIDS: ON THE INSIDE LOOKING OUT AFTER LOSS also provides a trauma specific interview process. It assists you in giving traumatized children the opportunity to find relief from their terror. It provides an opportunity to better cope with the posttraumatic reactions that can put a stranglehold on their psychosocial, cognitive and emotional development.

The appendix includes important information for parents about their child's reactions to trauma. These segments reinforce that children are vulnerable to posttraumatic stress and all its reactions, reactions that are in addition to and different from grief reactions.

KIDS is the result of over 200 traumatic specific interviews with children 3 - 16 years of age from a seven county area in Southeastern Michigan, an economically and culturally diverse area. The staff involved presented both violent and non-violent incidents that induced moderate to severe levels of trauma. Their experiences clearly established that children not only are eager but they need to confront the details of their trauma.

The format of *KIDS* does the following:

1. Increases awareness about trauma reactions children can experience;

2. Demonstrates the ways children view themselves and their life following traumatic experiences;

3. Dispels myths related to children being "too young" to experience posttraumatic stress, being resilient, and being able to "outgrow" their trauma experience;

4. Details a trauma specific interview process and assists you in using this approach; and,

5. Provides information that can be shared and made available to parents to educate them about the needs of their traumatized child.

Our hope is that *KIDS: ON THE INSIDE LOOKING OUT AFTER LOSS* will bring to you and the children you work with many of the same benefits we saw.

The Institute for Trauma and Loss in Children (TLC) is a nonprofit organization established in 1990. It is largely a volunteer organization. TLC's mission is to bring to those who work with children and families the knowledge, resources and skills necessary to help children and families exposed to violent and nonviolent traumatic losses.

Collectively, you who participate in TLC trainings or use TLC resources are working with thousands of traumatized children and families each year. Only through you can we have an impact on their lives.

We encourage your feedback. Please write or call us about any of the TLC resources or trainings you attend. We promise your comments, suggestions, and information will be incorporated into our resources and trainings so we can continue to provide you with timely and practical resources and strategies.

If our materials or trainings have been helpful, please tell others. Your referrals are far more valuable than a flyer in the mail.

Thank you for your support. The problems children and families are presenting are themselves traumatic and difficult to face day after day without our supporting each others' efforts.

❤ ❤ ❤ ❤ ❤ ❤ ❤ ❤

TLC staff are available for consultation and training in the areas of violence prevention, intervention and postvention, Crisis Response Teams, violent or non--violent student/staff death, and debriefing staff following traumatic events such as suicide, homicide and other traumatic events..

For further information call or write:

TLC INSTITUTE
c/o Bill Steele
20171 Mack Avenue
Grosse Pointe Woods, MI 48236
(313) 885-0390

HISTORICAL ACCOMPLISHMENTS SINCE 1990

- Over 300,000 children have been exposed to TLC programs.
- Over 1,500 schools nationally are using TLC programs.
- Over 20,000 educators have participated in TLC trainings.
- Working with Families in Crisis, a book written by TLC co-founder published in 1991 by Guilford Publishing, New York, for use by educators and school counselors.
- Traumatic and Troubling Losses for Children: Individual and Organized Interventions, text, published in 1992 by TLC Institute for use by educators and school counselors.
- After a Loss: Thoughts, Verbalizations, Feelings and Behaviors, a booklet published in 1992 by TLC for use by survivors and counselors.
- Successful first, second and third "Where Have All the Children Gone?" annual conferences, attended by 385 professionals.
- Depression and Stress content writers for Club Connect, City for Youth, Channel 56, PBS television show aired in October, 1992.
- Depression and stress school curriculum writers including videotape for Club Connect, TV 56, December, 1992. Distributed nationally.

- First Americans invited by the Kuwait Government to train the counselors or its newly formed Social Development Office on ways to work with families traumatized by the war, 1993.

- Exclusive contract to provide PTSD related training and counseling in Europe, signed, 1993.

- Produced (June, 1993) 68 minute videotape, Children of Trauma: Tools to Help the Helper. Actual interviews with 6, 11, and 15 year old siblings of sister murdered by serial killer Leslie Williams. The interviews demonstrate the power of drawing as both as assessment tool and a therapeutic relief of symptoms induced by their trauma.

- Alternatives to Fighting and Suspension, a conflict resolution program for middle school and junior high school students. Published in 1993 by TLC Institute.

For a complete catalog of these resources and other helpful materials, please contact:

KIDSRIGHTS
10100 Park Cedar Drive
Charlotte, NC 28210
800/892-5437 or 704/541-0100
fax 704/541-0113

1

TRAUMATIC LOSSES, TRAUMATIC REACTIONS

We all know that children experience grief when they suffer the loss of someone close to them either by death, divorce or separation.

But, when that loss also traumatizes a child, they experience additional reactions that are quite different from normal grief reactions.

Let's look at how a happy, non-traumatized child sees herself.

This is a happy, non-traumatized four year old's drawing of herself. We see a child who is happy, has a personality. Her picture is strong, well defined. This is how she looks at herself and her world.

What happens to a happy child who has been traumatized?

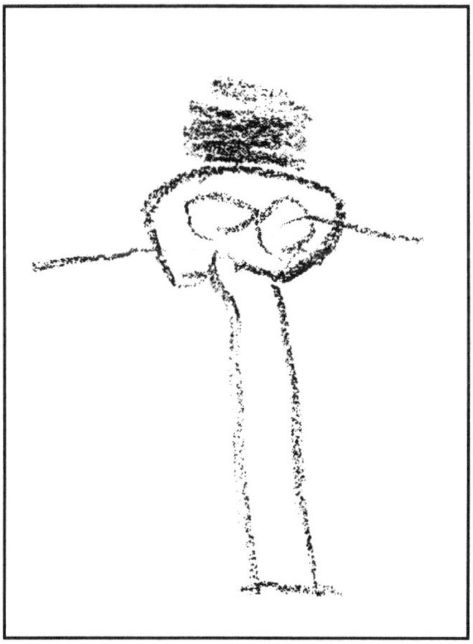

This too is a self portrait drawn by a four year old. This child witnessed the rape of her mother. Notice how weak her drawing is when we compare it to that of the non-traumatized child. There are no definitive legs, feet or hands. Without legs and feet she can't run, can't stand her ground. Without hands she can't fight back or reach out and grab on. It is almost as if the child is malformed, incomplete. The eyes are hollow as if life has been stolen from them or what she sees in her world is too awful to look at. This is a terrorized child. As an adult it is so much easier to believe that children are safe, that they are immune to overwhelming terror. However, we know that what they draw is what they see and how they feel. We also know that sometimes we can look at children from the outside and they seem to "look" as if they are doing okay. But, for the child on the inside looking out, the picture can be quite different.

A child exposed to violence, such as a witness to murder, assault, domestic violence, is likely to be traumatized. Yet an event, does not need to be violent to leave a child traumatized.

This is a drawing by a four-year-old child following the divorce of his parents. Not every divorce will leave a child traumatized, yet many do. The loss of a parent or the parent(s)' behavior during or after the divorce can leave a child terrorized. We see remarkable similarities with these last two children's drawings because of the terror they experienced, one because of witnessing such a violent event, the other because of losing a parent.

Terror is what distinguishes a traumatic reaction from a grief reaction. (You may want to share these three drawings with parents to help them appreciate what their child may be experiencing).

CHILDREN ARE VULNERABLE

Often many parents as well as professionals in the position to help traumatized children fail to recognize that children are vulnerable to the kinds of posttraumatic stress once attributed only to adults survivors of war. Many still believe children are too young, too unknowing to be seriously affected. Many minimize the reactions of children and believe they'll "grow out of it". Others simply do not know what to look for or fail to recognize changes in the child as symptoms of posttraumatic stress.

What kinds of event can induce trauma in children?

- separation from a parent due to the parent's substance abuse problems, physical/sexual abuse, neglect or abandonment
- the murder of a sibling, parent or friend
- the witnessing of the killing of a sibling, parent or friend, including the witnessing of a suicide
- the discovery of a body
- witnessing a rape, physical abuse of family member or friend
- death of a family member by fire, car accident, drowning, plane or train crash, or from a hurricane, tornado, flood or earthquake.
- terminal illness and death of a family member or peer
- divorce
- adoption
- neither witnessing nor actually being involved in any of the above but simply being a friend or peer of someone who has died, been killed or committed suicide.

WHEN CHILDREN ARE TRAUMATIZED

Both violent and non-violent events that involve a threat to one's life or a loss of someone else's life would be distressing to almost anyone. Posttraumatic stress disorder and the experiencing of the horrific terror it can produce can overwhelm children.

(Appendix includes this material for copying.)

When a child is terrorized, what happens? A child may

- ❍ have trouble sleeping because of nightmares
- ❍ be afraid to sleep alone or be left alone even for short periods of time
- ❍ be easily startled (terrorized) by sounds, sights, smells similar to those that existed at the time of the event. A car backfiring may sound like the gun shot that killed someone. For one child his dog pouncing down the stairs brought back the sound of his father falling down the stairs and dying
- ❍ become hypervigilant, forever watching out for and anticipating that they are about to be or are in danger. (Children who start sleeping on the floor instead of their bed after a trauma do so because they fear the comfort of a bed will let them sleep so hard they won't be able to hear the danger coming)
- ❍ become irritable, aggressive, act tough, provoke fights or
- ❍ verbalize a desire for revenge
- ❍ act as if they are no longer afraid of anything or anyone (and in face of danger not respond appropriately), verbalize that nothing ever scares them anymore
- ❍ forget recently acquired skills
- ❍ return to behaviors they had previously stopped, i.e., bed wetting, nail biting, or develop disturbing behaviors, i.e., stuttering

- withdraw and want less to do with their friends
- develop headaches, stomach problems, fatigue and other ailment not previously present
- become accident prone, take risks they previously avoided, put themselves in life threatening situations
- develop school behavior problems including a drop in grades and difficulty concentrating
- develop a pessimistic view of the future, lose their resilience to overcome additional difficulties, lose hope, lose their passion to survive, play, enjoy life

While these changes are not unusual they often go unnoticed or fail to bring a helping response from adults. These changes can and do become permanent when the child does not receive appropriate help. Often children suffer silently for years with their terror, until one or several of these changes become so intense and problematic that someone says something. Unfortunately, years later few people are likely to associate these reactions to the child's earlier trauma. The help given often misses the mark. This further increases the child's sense of helplessness and failure.

How Is Trauma Different?

1. Trauma reactions are in addition to the normal grief reactions that follow a loss -- shock, disbelief, denial, anger, sadness and the eventual acceptance of the loss.
2. Trauma reactions, however, often overpower grief reactions and NOT UNTIL the trauma induced terror is overcome do the above grief reactions begin to emerge.

3. Although there are no definitive time lines, most individuals move through their grief reactions, accept the loss and begin to live life fully again in one or two years. When that loss is traumatic, traumatic reactions can continue for years. Often times the trauma can be buried, forgotten for several years and all its reactions suddenly triggered. During this time grief reactions also remain buried.

4. Children do not just "grow out" of their trauma, not without help. They need help from parents who have the knowledge to recognize and understand what their child is experiencing and the tools to support them as they deal with their terror. And, at times, they need help from trained professionals.

Once we see what the traumatized child sees, we understand how critical it is to give them the opportunity to confront the details of their trauma.

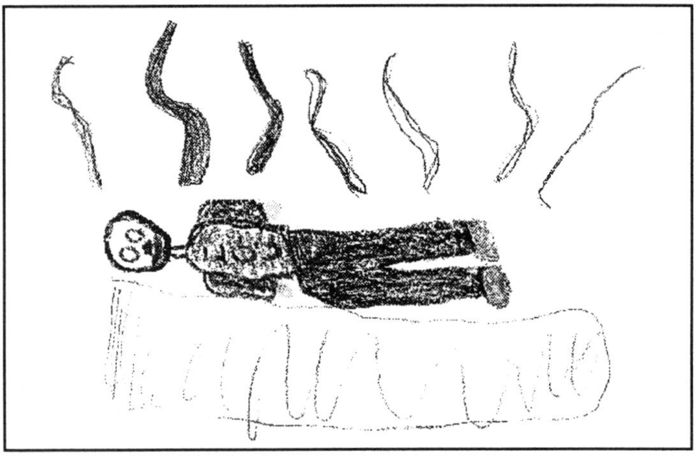

This 15 year old's drawing of his sister's body is filled with terror. Traumatized children come face to face with terror. It is the terror they experience that leads to a drastic, often horrifying change in the self image and view of life they held before the experience.

Why is it so important to know what images and fantasies have taken over the child's life since the terror he experienced? Claudia Jewett, author of *Helping Children Cope with Separation and Loss* (1992), tells the following story about Robert whom at age four was released for adoption. Years later when given the opportunity to share the fantasies he had developed after that traumatic separation, he said this about being born:

> Robert: Not me. I didn't grow in a mom.
>
> Helper: You didn't? That's fascinating. You're the first kid I ever met who didn't get born that way. How was it instead?
>
> Robert: You see, what happened was one day my social worker was feeling like having a snack. She opened a box of crackerjacks. She looked inside and pulled me out. She said, "You're no prize!" and put me in the trash.

A child who sees himself as trash, as a "throwaway" will behave like trash and fully expect to be tossed away, ignored, go unwanted.

It is critical to accept that children can indeed be traumatized. The terror they experience transforms their image of themselves and of those around them into portraits of terror, powerlessness, worthlessness, helplessness, haplessness and hopelessness.

Robert's story is not unlike the stories of other traumatized children who have been victimized by physical/sexual assault, witnessed violence in the home, lost a loved one to a traumatic accident, abandonment, divorce, separation.

Generally parents are able to comfort children who are grieving. They have learned to be patient and tolerant and understand that grieving children need time too. Trauma reactions are so different and unfamiliar that parents attribute them to other problems. It's very easy to become frustrated and angry when you don't know that children are experiencing traumatic reactions they have no control over. Nor will they gain control and find relief without help. When parents and other trusted adults fail to know or do not understand how children react to trauma, they often respond in a way that makes it even more difficult for the child.

How children respond to a traumatic loss is something we all need to learn about if we are to help children find relief from their terror.

Reading the stories of traumatized children, looking at their drawings and seeing how they view themselves and life can help us understand the terror that children can experience.

2

CHILDREN OF TRAUMA: THEIR STORIES

The following stories and drawings are the result of using a very trauma specific, structured interview that covered only one session. The children themselves determined the length of the session that went from approximately thirty minutes to as long as ninety minutes.

The interview process, which will be detailed later in the book, consists of trauma specific questions and the use of drawing. It provides a comfortable medium for children to express themselves. The ages of the children/youth ranged from 3 - 16 years of age. The amount of lapsed time from the actual trauma experience to these interviews ranged from one to seven years, although a few interviews occurred within weeks of the event.

The incidents cover violent and non-violent events. During the some 200 interviews conducted, our counselors found that the children, when given the opportunity were eager to talk about the details of their trauma. Previous counselors had never asked most of these children the trauma specific questions asked in these interviews. Nor had most counselors asked the children to draw specific pictures of their experiences. The parents who fortunately observed these interviews found the kinds of images their children carried with them both amazing and alarming. The drawing process elicited feelings and memories their child had not communicated to them. This surprised them. The questions we asked were questions they might have thought about asking but were afraid to ask. Their children's responses also surprised them. By observing their children, parents began to see them differently and appreciate how their child was, in fact, affected by their trauma experience. Afterward parents generally were more responsive to counselor suggestions.

The counselors who conducted these interviews had a minimum of five (5) years of experience working with children, including traumatized children. Unfortunately, the counselors were never trained in trauma specific intervention so the children they had previously seen did not benefit from this structured process. The counselors reported that this process actually lowered their anxiety. It gave them direction and a structured format that was still flexible enough to help the child who refused to draw. They found that the children they had been seeing began to share information they had never shared before. They found that the process, though at times emotionally difficult provided the child with a vehicle for finding some relief from their terror. It also helped them to recapture some sense of control over the effects of their trauma -- a critical step for moving from victim to survivor.

The process also identified areas that would most certainly need continued attention, more attention than could be provided in one session. Counselors, however, reported that even if the parents did not bring the children back, they felt this process helped to increase the child's sense of empowerment. It provided them with new ways to cope with the trauma reactions they might experience. It provided them with a greater understanding that given their experience their reactions were not at all unusual; information that was also very valuable for parents.

SURVIVOR OF A FAMILY MEMBER'S MURDER

What are the differences in reactions between those who actually witness a murder and those who do not witness but have a loved one, family member murdered?

Following are the brief stories of Elizabeth, six years old, Tommy, 11 years old, and Mary, 15 years old. A serial killer abducted, raped and murdered their 15 year old sister. He buried her body that was not found until six months after the murder. The boyfriend witnessed the abduction but survived the attack. *(These three interviews are part of the Children of Trauma videotape. See back of book for more details).*

NAME: ELIZABETH
AGE AT INCIDENT: 5
AGE SEEN BY TLC: 6

CURRENT TRAUMA REACTIONS:

Plays less
Much more anxious, moody and aggressive
Experiences intrusive images, thoughts
Has bad dreams
Startle reactions
Impaired concentration
Started sleep walking
Sucking her thumb, biting her nails
Sleeps on the floor
Started getting into fights

Elizabeth was extremely shy, not the outgoing, playful, confident, little girl her mom describes before her sister's murder. Her replies were very brief and the counselor had to ask her for further explanation. She wanted mom to sit close to her. She sat unusually still during the interview, constricted not only in her speech but also in her body movements. Her responses were at the level of a whisper, at times difficult for the interviewer to hear clearly.

When I asked Elizabeth to draw a picture she could tell a story about, she immediately drew a face, her face, but she could not talk about any aspects of the face. When I asked her where her body was, she said, "No where." When I asked her to draw her body, she drew herself with no feet. She approached drawing a picture of her murdered sister, Cindy, in the same manner. Remember the drawing by the four year old who had witnessed her mother's rape? Feet and hands were missing, suggesting helplessness and powerlessness.

In the early part of this interview Elizabeth expresses a sense of helplessness and powerlessness in the way she presented herself and in her drawings. Interestingly, when I asked her to draw any picture she'd like to tell a story about, she decided to draw herself, suggesting attention focus on her.

Her helplessness emerged dramatically when I asked her to draw a picture of her family. (Elizabeth, 1)

ELIZABETH 1

From left to right she drew mom, Mary, her older sister, and Tommy, her older brother. She completely left out her younger four-year-old sister with whom she had been fighting with frequently over the past six months. She also left herself out.

In response to my question, "Where are you?" she showed the most spontaneity and animation since the interview began. She took her finger and placed it on her drawing of mom and said with a smile and a strong voice, "I'm here." "Where is here?" I asked. "My mommy's belly," she replied.

ELIZABETH 2

From that point on Elizabeth talked about what it was like to be a baby. When I later asked her to draw herself, she drew herself as a baby (Elizabeth, 2), again with no feet, no hands.

After the interview Elizabeth's mother told us that she hadn't realized how much Elizabeth needed to be nurtured and pampered. Nor had she realized how helpless and powerless Elizabeth was feeling. This was contrary to her aggressive, somewhat independent behavior. Mom had thought Elizabeth's behavior meant she was feeling quite differently.

The interview with Elizabeth lasted approximately 25 minutes. Elizabeth had seen previous counselors, but again, this trauma specific approach was not utilized. Yet, as Elizabeth's mother and we can support, this approach yielded a very different identity than Elizabeth had been carrying around since her sister's murder, an identity that her behavior did not reflect, and therefore one that had gone unattended.

NAME: TOMMY
AGE AT INCIDENT: 10
AGE SEEN BY TLC: 11

CURRENT TRAUMA REACTIONS:

- Extremely anxious and frightened
- Extremely shy
- Lacking confidence
- Startle reactions

Initially, Tommy had a very difficult time talking about what had happened to his sister. At times he gagged on his words and had to make a strong, concentrated effort to get them out. Tears came within five minutes of the start of the interview. After spending some time talking about the actual details of the killing I asked him to draw a picture he could tell a story about. (Tommy, 1)

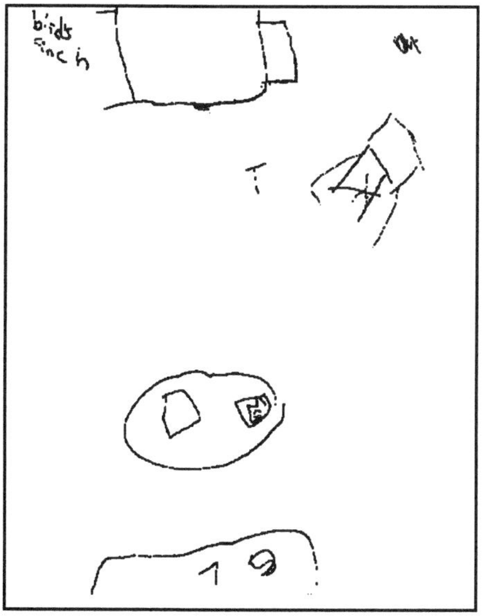

TOMMY 1

His drawing is primitive and yet he spent a good 20 minutes describing the events of the last evening he had spent with his sister. This is actually the drawing of his living room where Tommy, his sister and her boyfriend had watched television and eaten a snack the night she left and never returned.

TOMMY 2

In a later drawing (Tommy, 2) drew a picture of himself that he identified was himself before Cindy's murder. When I asked him whether he was smiling in the drawing he tried to turn the mouth into a smile but could not.

Since he drew a picture of himself before the incident, I asked him to draw one following his sister's death. (Tommy, 3) Again, while he was drawing, he continued to talk about a variety of feelings, incidents, and concerns.

Notice his arms in the "after drawing". They're huge. He referred to them as "like Freddie Kreuger's." His portrayal of himself before and after is interesting as his mother described him before the murder as generally calm, somewhat shy, but very confident. Afterward he became extremely anxious and frightened, shy and not at all confident. As the only boy in a family of three sisters and no father, he may now feel an exaggerated need to protect his mother and sisters.

TOMMY 3

His drawing of himself afterward as happy, strong, a force to be reckoned with also could be more a reflection of what he might have been before his sister's murder, and the "before" drawing how he currently feels but cannot portray.

In the past no one asked Tommy to draw his sister's body, yet this difficult task is one that children often later point to as most helpful. The picture he drew (Tommy, 4) is a frightening image.

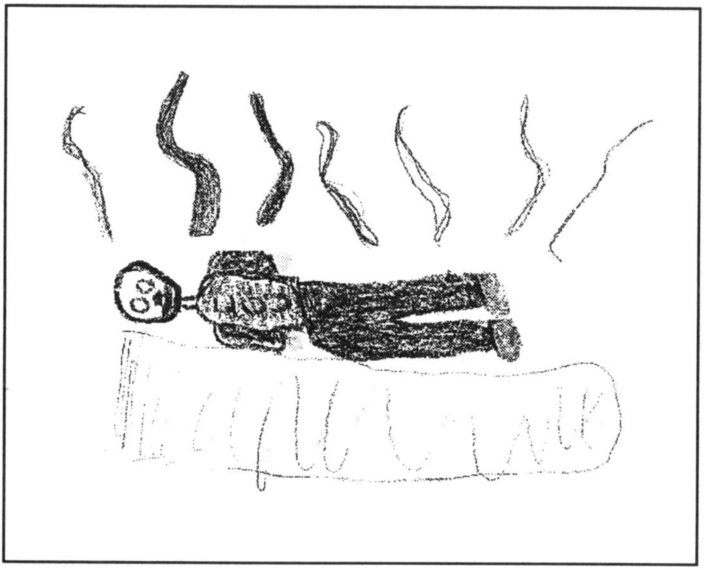

TOMMY 4

The interview lasted approximately 90 minutes. In the process of concluding the interview Tommy spontaneously began to draw (Tommy, 5) how he still felt on the inside a year later. He initially described this as "like melted pizza" and then added, "It's as if Candyman was reaching inside and pulling your guts out." This last reference helped his mother realize that Tommy was less in control of his terror than she had thought. She also realized that he too needed a different response from her.

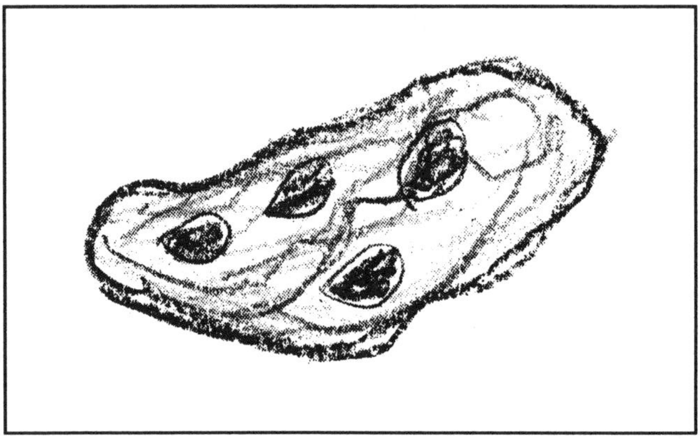

TOMMY 5

The change in Tommy from the beginning of the interview when he could barely get a word out and cried spontaneously while giving details, revealed still very intense pain. By the end of the interview, however, he easily could have continued. He was initiating new issues, telling us about other experiences, was very articulate, and was even laughing. Though initially difficult, Tommy had released much of his pain and found relief.

No one had ever asked him to use drawing to describe details of the event and his reactions to it. When I asked him what he had found to be most helpful, he stated, "Drawing made it easier than just talking."

NAME: MARY
AGE AT INCIDENT: 14
AGE SEEN BY TLC: 15

CURRENT TRAUMA REACTIONS:

"No fear" attitude
Poor choice of friends
Constant fighting with her mother
Emotional detachment

Three children, all in one family, yet they all reacted differently to their sister's murder. One year later they are still reacting differently.

One year later Mother's greatest concerns with Mary were her "no fear" attitude, the carelessness in the type of friends she chose and the constant fighting between Mary and her mother.

When I asked Mary about her relationship with her mother before and after her sister's murder, she had no trouble expressing her current frustration and anger. When I eventually asked her about her own feelings and feeling about her dead sister, she became emotionally detached.

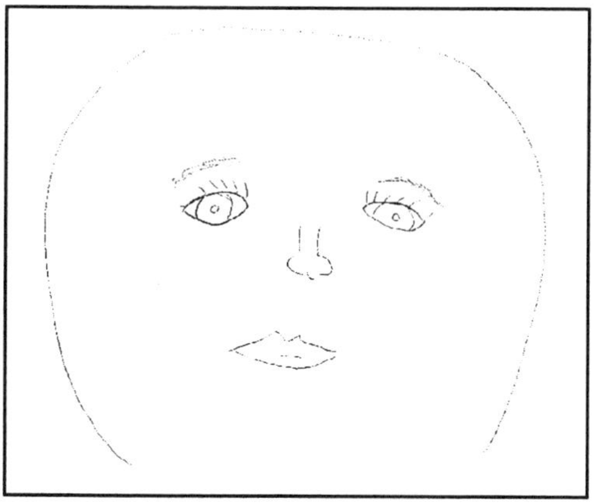

MARY 1

Following the drawing (Mary, 1) of her face I asked her what she saw. She responded that she "needed more eye makeup." When I pushed her to describe what the face expressed, she simply didn't know. When I asked her about memories of her sister, she responded that she really didn't think about her. When I asked her about her dreams for the future, she could not describe what she thought she might like to do. She said that she didn't think about it. When I asked her if there is anything now that upsets her or scares her, she replied, "Nothing really phases me."

In essence Mary had emotionally detached herself or deadened her feelings during the past year, except her struggle with her mother whom she said, "wants me to do and be like Cindy." Also since her sister's death she had placed herself at risk via her association and behavior with this "new" crowd.

Approximately 40 minutes into the interview I asked her to draw a picture of what happened the night her sister never returned home. At first she said that she couldn't draw this. I used stick figures to prove that how it looked didn't matter. What did matter was her attempt to put all that happened into a drawing (Mary, 2). I suggested she just begin with drawing a part of her sister's car, such as the wheels.

MARY 2

She drew a stick figure of the killer and then Cindy standing next to the car. Mary then began tracing Cindy's stick figure and answered one or two questions about how she had died. She became quiet, and starred intently at the drawing. Shortly afterward she began to cry. The more she cried, the more memories she had of her sister. It was the first time since Cindy's funeral that she had cried. She went from being very emotionally detached to reclaiming her feelings. Trauma specific questions and drawing, even primitive details of the event and the people involved, helped break through her detachment.

When we give children and adolescents the opportunity to confront the details of trauma they do respond and express their gratitude.

SEXUAL VICTIMIZATION BY ANOTHER YOUTH

NAME: DANIEL
AGE AT INCIDENT: 5
AGE SEEN BY TLC: 5 (1 month after incident)

CURRENT TRAUMA REACTIONS:

- Irritable
- Frequent loss of temper
- Regressed to baby talk
- Afraid to be alone/clings
- Sucks his thumb
- Headaches

DANIEL 1

Daniel was sexually victimized by his teenage cousin. When his mother learned of this she sought help. At the point in the interview when the counselor asked him to draw a picture of himself, he could not. Daniel, 1 is the result of his attempt.His identity is lost in chaos, broken into pieces, scattered, not identifiable as even living. This is a reflection of what terror can do to a child's sense of person, his sense of identity.
Should one question his ability to draw a living representation of someone, Daniel, 2 is his drawing of his mother that he

DANIEL 2

drew during the same interview. Like Elizabeth, Daniel draws only a face, but he draws a face with a personality.

Daniel had no difficulty drawing what he wanted to happen to the person who hurt him. (Daniel, 3).

The perpetrator, an older boy, is the face at the bottom of the page. He is crying because Daniel's father, the top face, is beating him with a belt. In Daniel's situation, loss of control over his anger emerged after this situation, yet no one had asked him what he would like to see happen to the perpetrator.

DANIEL 3

Two sessions later, when the counselor asked Daniel to try again and draw a picture of himself, he produced a response of hope. (Daniel, 4)

(The purpose of drawing is not to obtain material to analyze. Any single drawing can have a multitude of interpretations. The purpose is to engage the child in a

DANIEL 4

safe, psychomotor activity that can elicit buried reactions and provide a safe vehicle for expressing their terror and sharing the details of their experience. The anticipated outcomes are that the child experiences relief from that terror and gains a renewed sense of power and empowerment over the terror that posttraumatic reactions induce). During the drawing process Daniel found this new identity,and talked about feeling better because of how his mother and father had fortunately responded to the incident and to the family members involved.

SEXUAL VICTIMIZATION BY PARENT

NAME: UNKNOWN
AGE AT INCIDENT: 7
AGE SEEN BY TLC: 8

CURRENT TRAUMA REACTIONS:

- Extremely anxious
- Fearful, hypervigilant
- Extremely moody, irritable, defiant
- Easily loses his temper
- Regressed to baby talk
- Intrusive images
- Traumatic dreams
- Sleep disturbances, enuresis, sleep walking
- Headaches

Father sexually victimized him several times. Though he had received previous counseling his drawing still depicts an overpowering monster in the boy's life, his father. (Figure 1)

He is actually sitting in a chair by the table in the lower right hand corner of the drawing. There are no discernable features. It's almost impossible to see an actual figure. An identity other than terror no longer exists.

Though his father is serving time, the terror remains. In the course of a single interview this child drew seven different drawings where he included himself, be we never see his face or facial features such as eyes. We see only a heart that the child often draws as a "broken heart." (Figure 2)

When the counselor asked him what he would like to see happen to his father, he said, "Die, because if he goes to prison he could escape or get let out." The need for empowerment, control over his terror still emerges one year later as a critical need for this child.

FIGURE 1

FIGURE 2

PHYSICAL ABUSE BY PARENT/SUBSEQUENT TRAUMAS

CONFIDENTIAL ASSUMED NAME: JEFFRY
AGE AT INCIDENT: 8
AGE SEEN BY TLC: 11

CURRENT TRAUMA REACTIONS:

Difficulty concentrating
Irritability
Outbursts of anger
Violent dreams

Jeffry was in a residential setting when provided a trauma specific interview. Prior to placement he had three school suspensions, was truant, had many fights, was said to exhibit attention deficit disorder at home and school.

From age two through seven, Jeffry suffered repeated physical abuse and neglect. His mother was also a substance abuser whose behavior was inconsistent and unpredictable. He was frequently locked in his room, or in closets. He was sometimes tied up when physically abused.

At age seven, Jeffry ran away from home and was eventually placed in Foster Care. After a period of time in the Foster Care Home he was placed with his grandparents. Shortly after this he was placed in a psychiatric residential setting. Following the psychiatric setting he was placed in a children's residential setting.

During his stay in the residential setting (approximately two years) he was very subdued. It was difficult to have any conversation related to his terrorizing experiences. As far as could be determined he had never been assessed for chronic posttraumatic stress and according to Jeffry never asked to draw about his experiences.

The multiple traumas experienced by Jeffry - bodily abuse, abandonment, out of home placement, out of control substance abusing parent, placement in psychiatric setting, etc. certainly would indicate symptoms in addition to PTSD.

The fascinating aspect of this interview, however, was the way in which Jeffry for the first time interacted with spontaneity and responsiveness to issues about his past traumatization. Once he was asked to draw and tell stories about his drawings he began to communicate and exhibit an energy quite different than the previous non-responsive, very subdued sessions.

JEFFRY 1

The first drawing (Jeffry, 1) is that of himself, and the house he lives in now. He provided details of what the house looked like as he drew. The drawings are primitive. The self portrait is incomplete and almost appears as if he has wings and is floating in the air. It was apparent that drawing was far easier for him than sitting and answering direct questions. Again there could be many different interpretations given to this first drawing. That is not, however, the purpose: the purpose is to engage the child in a psychomotor process that can facilitate later relief from trauma related terror.

In the second drawing (Jeffry, 2) he drew a picture of the camper where his mother's boyfriend lived. The camper was often in the driveway. As he finishes the camper and begins to describe one of the traumatic incidents he experienced, he begins to doodle to the left of the camper. He retraces and repeatedly colors in one section while describing the details of the event. There were a variety of colors he could choose from, he chose red.

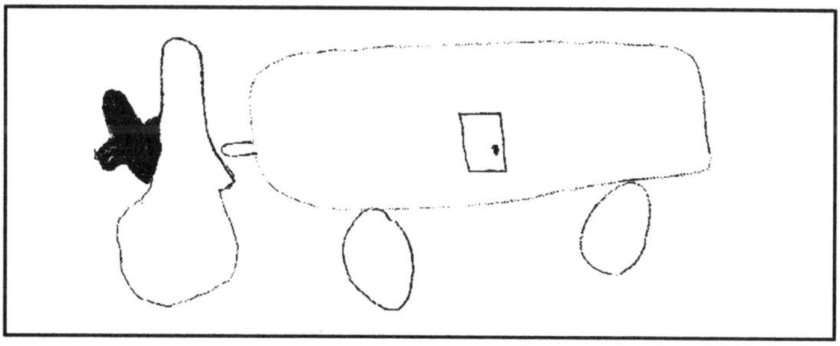

JEFFRY 2

The third drawing (Jeffry, 3) was the result of being asked to draw a specific incident, that was very frightening to him. The drawing is of the time his mother got very angry (she is the bigger figure). Jeffry was not sure why she was so mad, but ran out of the house because he was so terrified of her. She screamed to him to come back but he wouldn't. She ran out after him. When she caught him, she put a knife to his throat.

JEFFRY 3

The mother's boyfriend was in the camper. Jeffry yelled but he never came out to help. His mother eventually let him go. He ran to his room immediately.

Notice the long black cloud he draws across the paper. Jeffry wished he could have taken the knife away from his mother at the time and "thrown it where she couldn't get it."

JEFFRY 4

Jeffry reported that nothing scares him anymore yet in his final drawing (Jeffry, 4), he draws a picture of a monster while describing more details and begins to share recurring dreams. He is a police officer killing people who break the law.

Because of the multiple placements, multiple traumas and multiple diagnoses given over the years assigning PTSD criteria becomes difficult.

What does emerge, however, as a result of this trauma specific process is not only new information for the worker, but a relationship that did not exist previously. Jeffry becomes much more involved and more giving in past sessions. He in fact, focuses on trauma detail not shared previously. In addition, the process assisted the worker in defining a focus of attention for subsequent sessions as well as reinforcing the use of drawing as a effective communication link to the child.

PRESENT DURING DROWNING OF SISTER

NAME: SHANNON
AGE AT INCIDENT: 7
AGE SEEN BY TLC: 7 (3 months later)

CURRENT TRAUMA REACTIONS:

Avoidance behavior (not wanting to talk)
Startle reaction
Survivor guilt

As indicated earlier, a non-violent incident can cause traumatic reactions. Acute stress occurs the first four weeks following such a traumatic event followed by PTSD, if these reactions persist.

SHANNON 1

At the time of the interview the Shannon's only sensory memory is her mother's yell when she saw that the inner tube her daughter had been in was empty. Her daughter was at the bottom of the pool, unconscious. She died within twenty-four hours at the hospital.

When the counselor asked Shannon to draw a picture of her sister she drew her in her favorite outfit, one she wore all the time. (Shannon, 1)

In the next drawing (Shannon, 2) she drew her sister in her bathing suit. While she drew this picture she supplied vivid, visual details. When the counselor asked her what she wished would have happened differently, her chin trembled and her lip quivered. She said wished she would have caught her sister.

SHANNON 2

We know that the younger the child is, the greater the need to avoid the traumatic aspects of the event. Her drawing shows her sister smiling, as did 6 year old Elizabeth's drawing of her dead sister. Yet the reality is that traumatic reactions cannot be avoided. As Shannon grows older, other reactions will begin to emerge.

At only 3 months after the event it is difficult to know what post-traumatic reactions might yet occur. Shannon is in a support group with other children whose brothers or sisters have died. Because she can share the details of her experience her survivor guilt and other trauma reactions that have developed during the past few months may not have as much impact as seen in those children who have not received trauma specific assistance.

DIVORCE

NAME: CONFIDENTIALITY MAINTAINED
(ASSIGNED NAME: PAUL)
AGE AT INCIDENT: 10
AGE SEEN BY TLC: 12

CURRENT TRAUMA REACTIONS:

Disruptive behavior in school
Sullen at home
No communication with family members
Emotional detachment

Paul's parents divorced two years ago. His mother has since remarried. Approximately two months ago Paul began displaying the above mentioned behaviors which brought them to counseling.

NOTE: It is quite common for reactions to emerge two years after the incident. In fact, during TLC's work in Kuwait after the Gulf War, most traumatic reactions were beginning to surface after two years .

Divorce does not always induce trauma reactions, but it certainly can.

When asked to draw his family doing an activity together, Paul asked, "Which family?" He decided to draw his family with his stepfather in it. (Paul, 1).

Paul drew his mother at the far right, his stepfather at the left, and his sister is the the most prominent figure we can see.

He drew "things" in the picture with much detail, but family members have no distinct facial features, are vague beings, almost phantom-like.

PAUL 1

Paul feels closest to his sister, and indeed, drew his sister as the most visible figure in the picture, but still with no identity.

The counselor did not conduct a trauma specific interview with Paul during this session. Paul may be experiencing more depression and stress than posttraumatic reactions, yet a trauma specific interview might reveal the existence of trauma. If you recall, in Chapter One there is a self-portrait of a four year old traumatized by divorce. There are no faces in Paul's drawing nor can we identify gender identities by simply looking at the drawing. As in six-year-old Elizabeth's drawing, Paul leaves himself out of the drawing. We do know that when the counselor asked Paul to provide a story with the drawing, he focused on all the details of the room as opposed to figures of the family members. Like Mary, he could not make an emotional connection to the figures. Those similarities certainly suggest a need for a trauma specific interview.

FATAL CAR ACCIDENT/MOTHER'S DEATH

NAME: B. J.
AGE AT INCIDENT: 13
AGE SEEN BY TLC: 16

CURRENT TRAUMA REACTIONS:

- Avoidance behavior
- Survivor guilt
- Cognitive disturbances
- Intrusive images
- Loss of control over anger

B. J.'s mother was killed in a car accident while she was driving her car. B. J. was not in the car. While we are unable to provide specific details of the accident; B.J. based his drawing on some information he had heard. The drawing depicts his visualization of the accident. The drawing (B.J., 1) by itself is not as important as the feelings that emerged during the process of B.J.'s attempt to draw his mother in the car.

Survivor guilt emerged as a major concern, a concern that had not previously emerged. Having this 16 year old visually focus on this specific detail made it easier for him to discuss his reactions and feelings which probably would have remained submerged in a question and answer format.

The therapist who used this process wrote, "As a therapist I have used a variety of tools to assist my clients ages 12-18 in discussing various losses. None has come close, however, to the process you have provided . . .We both found it to be one of the most insightful methods for getting at the core of feelings and reactions following traumatic losses."

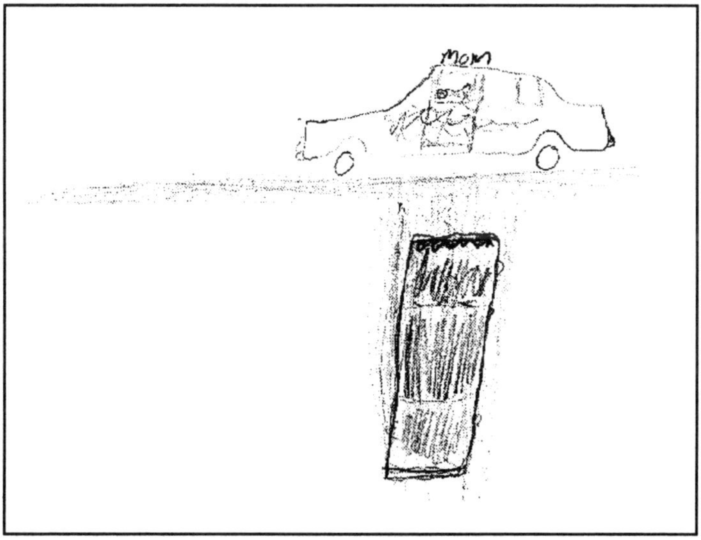

B.J. 1

SUMMARY

Knowing what questions to ask and how to help children focus on the details of their trauma benefit both the child and those of you who work with traumatized children.

3

THE INTERVIEW PROCESS WITH CHILDREN

Who Is Vulnerable?

Research related to PTSD and Children accelerated in the mid 80s with Eth and Pynoos' 1985 book, *Post Traumatic Stress Disorder in Children.* Today there is no doubt that children are vulnerable to PTSD following both violent and nonviolent events. We identified these events in Chapter One. Trauma specialists Pynoos (1985), Terr (1991), Clarke (1993), Stuber (1991), Yale (1990), Saigh (1991), and March, (1993) identified those events as capable of inducing PTSD in children. The newly revised DSM-IV also identifies additional PTSD diagnostic criteria for children.

What we know about vulnerability or risk is:

1. PTSD correlates with the degree of exposure or proximity to the event (Pynoos, 1987). Those actually at the event ("most exposed") are at greater risk, yet those who are "least exposed" also can experience PTSD.

2. "Most Exposed" can be defined as being a victim, participant, or witness. "Least Exposed" can be defined as a relative, peer, friend who was not present at the traumatizing event.

3. Saigh (1991) found that exposure can be the result of verbal exposure -- hearing from survivors the details of their experience. This also has implications related to the stress of those who work with traumatized children every day. They, too, can begin to experience PTSD reactions over time.

4. Pynoos (1987) found that reactions do differ by exposure but not by sex, ethnicity or age. Every child is vulnerable.

Therefore, the answer to the question, "Who Is Vulnerable?" is everyone at the incident and everyone who is in some way associated with the participant(s) of the incident.

Given this information PTSD assessment should extend far beyond the most obvious, the victimized child or the child who witnessed a traumatic incident.

When Do We Interview?

This question has two implications. Can we interview too soon after the incident? Is there a period of time when a trauma specific focus is no longer effective?

- After an Australian brush fire disaster, McFarland (1987) found that eighteen (18) months later the prevalence of PSD symptom presence had not changed.
- Fourteen (14) months after a sniper attack at an elementary school left one child dead, Wader, et. al. (1990) reported that symptoms continued, especially in those children who had known the murdered child..
- In children undergoing a bone marrow transplant, PTSD symptoms existed up to twelve (12) months following the transplant.
- In a four (4) year follow-up with 25 school bus kidnapping victims and one child who narrowly missed the exposure, Terr (1983) revealed that every child exhibited effects of PTSD.
- In 1994 TLC assessed 176 children for PTSD symptoms and found PTSD symptoms up to ten (10) years after the incident.

We believe that a trauma specific interview is valuable to the child/adolescent whenever it becomes known that they experienced a potentially trauma inducing incident as a participant, witness, relative, friend or peer.

The one exception might be immediately following the incident. Malchiodi (1990) in her work with children brought by their mothers to domestic violence shelters found that children were understandably at the peak of crisis. Terror, anxiety, feelings of helplessness are often manifested in shock, withdrawal, the unwillingness to participate in any tasks, as if there has been a "shut down."

Basic nurturing and a sense of safety and security needed to be reestablished. She found that for most children this "shut down" generally passed within several hours. Others have found that some children are very verbal following incidents. Following a trauma a complex array of factors governs a child immediate responses. These factors need further study to determine if certain incidents cause shorter or longer delays in the child's ability to communicate the details of their trauma. However, we do know that children do have the capacity and desire to explore their traumatic experience (Pynoos, 1985) and that we must respond as soon as possible and until the child can revisit the details of the experience.

What Is An Effective Way For Children To Communicate These Details?

We have seen that there is an initial "shut down". Muteness or numbness is not unusual. Direct inquiry is generally unproductive. Hafern and Peterson (1982), Pynoos (1986) Malchiodi (1990) and others concur that such a crisis as trauma produces needs an indirect yet focused response. Most agree that most children can communicate feelings through drawing as opposed to words.

Why Drawing?

Engaging children in drawing "will help them to at least partially compensate for the tendency to become passive, helpless, and dependent during crises." (Malchiodi, 1990). Eth and Pynoos (1986) found that children "energetically" took to drawing even hours after witnessing a violent event. Keep in mind that children are already visualizing the incident in their minds. Drawing connects or builds a bridge to their visualizations. Drawings become actual details of the event or fantasy representations that the child may need as a defense against the overwhelming terror their trauma induces.

Drawing is a way of taking the terror out of the trauma. It is a way of defusing overwhelming feelings. (Levinson, 1986). Those who have used it with other trauma inducing incidents have found it very beneficial for the child.

Why Storytelling?

The natural complement of drawing is storytelling. Storytelling offers the child a "metaphorical license", the freedom to verbalize the details of their trauma in ways that are safe. Some will use metaphors, others will use the actual details of what took place. Children naturally begin to tell stories generally around three years of age. Storytelling also becomes a safe way for the child to defuse overwhelming feelings.

INTERVIEW -- CONSULTATION GOALS

Keep in mind that a traumatized child is a child in crisis. Providing unstructured art expression or allowing the child to tell rambling stories can increase their anxiety. The traumatized child needs structure and direction to help reclaim control over their runaway fears. They do not need to be given too many choices, unlimited, or unguided self-expression. This will only increase their fear and the maladaptive coping skills they generally adopt such as aggressive behavior, hyperagitation, attachment behavior, craving for attention anyway they can get it.

THE GOAL

The following interview -- consultation process is structured yet flexible enough to allow the child to direct its course within that structure. The goals of this single session process are:

1. Stabilization;
2. Assessment of child's adaptation;
3. Identification of PTSD reactions;
4. Provide child with an opportunity to revisit the trauma in the supportive, reassuring presence of adult (professional) who understands the value of providing this opportunity;

5. Provide child with an opportunity to find relief from their terror;

6. Provide child with an opportunity to reestablish a positive "connectiveness" to an adult to foster continued development;

7. To normalize current and future reactions;

8. To support child's heroic efforts to become a survivor, not a victim of their experience;

9. To restore to the child's sensory experience, a positive experience; and,

10. To identify additional needs and the role parents can take to help meet these needs.

"A picture is worth a thousand words." The use of the drawing process in this structured, trauma specific, single session -- consultation is worth the months of direct inquiry it could take to achieve the same outcome.

THE INTERVIEW

Materials:

Children of Trauma: Tools to Help the Helpers videotape (60 minutes, VHS) demonstrates this entire process. (See back of book for more information).

Pencils and paper. We do not suggest crayons although color pencils may be used. Pencils lend themselves to drawing finer details. Use a different sheet of paper for each drawing.

Step One: Structuring the Purpose

This process actually begins when you communicate to the child your experiences in helping children who have experienced similar situations and reactions. If this is your first use of this intervention process, you might indicate how interested you are in knowing what their experience was like so you can help other children who will be coming to you with similar situations. This structuring of the purpose of your meeting occurs after your normal introduction with children and families who you are seeing for the first time.

Step Two: The Drawing/Interview Process

Ask the child to draw a picture they can tell you a story about. (Adolescents 14 years of age and older may hesitate to draw at the beginning of the interview. Spend some time with questions and answers, a format they're accustomed to. Educate them about trauma, what it is, the reactions that occur, and the normalcy of these reactions. Once you have spent some time establishing the relationship and learning more about the event, move on to ask them to draw. With encouragement, even adults will make crude drawings).

If the child/adolescent resists drawing, there are several responses:

1. Draw several stick figures and show that this is what you were thinking they could draw. Be primitive with your drawings.

2. If they still resist, suggest they tell you what to draw on the paper. After drawing each item, ask them if they wish to change it. Give them the pencil to correct or add to what you have drawn. Encourage them at this point to continue drawing.

3. If the child says they want to play, set a time limit for playing with the agreement that after playing they will draw.

4. If they still resist, show them examples of what other children have drawn. Initially this may contaminate their drawing. Once the process begins however, the child will begin to draw upon their own hidden images, fantasies, memories.

Rather than continuing the passive, uninvolved, detached response of the traumatized child, drawing begins the process of engaging the child's active response to their terror. The child may draw a picture and tell a story that may not have anything to do with the trauma. Let them finish, then focus them on drawing a picture related to their experience.

Once the child begins drawing about the incident itself, be curious about every aspect of the drawing. Ask questions about the different aspects, i.e., "What is this line?" "Why is this circle bigger than that circle?" Your curiosity encourages the continued release of trauma material and helps engage them in the process.
If they draw small faces, ask them to draw the same face larger and on another sheet of paper. It they have not included themselves in their drawing, ask them where they are and have them draw themselves. Ask if anyone is not in the drawing and, if not, ask them to draw and tell you about the person.

As their story unfolds, you'll begin to develop a more comprehensive picture of the severity of their experience, their reactions to it, and their coping skills.

Possible Responses

Some children need to avoid the painful memories and will change the actual details or outcome of the incident. Some will leave out critical components such as their presence at the event. Others will focus specifically on one aspect of their reaction and continue repetitive themes related to that response, such as the fear of what might happen to them in the future.

Using the trauma specific questions we've listed helps you and the child remain focused on the incidents. The questions refer specifically to the event and the child's reactions to it. They take you and the child through the range of possible PTSD reactions.

Although we suggest an order to these questions, the child really needs the opportunity to direct you. As we stated earlier, some children will immediately move to the details of the trauma and it would be appropriate to ask them to draw the body of the victims. Other children, however, may begin with less direct attention to the detail of the trauma. Many children we interviewed began by drawing a picture of themselves when we asked them to draw a picture they could tell a story about. Obviously, the story related to themselves would be pursued and completed. Afterward, direct their attention to some aspect of the trauma and when it fits, attention to the victim.

Trauma Questions

(A list of questions without examples is at the back of the book for your use).

- What were you doing?
- Are there any sounds, smells, sights that you recall?

These may trigger the child's sensory memories, and may, in fact, startle the child months, even years later. One child who was present when the police were taking pictures of her mother's body still reacts two years later whenever someone sets off a flash. Another child, seven years of age, remembers that the radio was playing when her mother's screams woke her up. (The mother had just learned that her husband had been killed in a snowmobile accident). Similar sounds still frighten her. The sound of planes flying overhead still startles many of the children in Kuwait, but this only occurs when it accompanied by other sensory memories such as certain smells.

It helps to know the sensory reactions of children so you can help normalize these reactions for them. Explain why, even two years later, certain sights, sounds, smells trigger traumatic reminders.

For the child who was not actually involved in the event but is exposed because of their relationship to the participants, you can ask, What were you doing when you first heard what happened? What sounds, smells, sights do you recall?

- Who else was there?

Sometimes the child leaves out critical players because they trigger overpowering feelings. The answer to this question can also explain current behaviors. Five teens were sitting on a porch when a friend came and sat with them. Shortly after that he pulled out a gun, put it to his head and killed himself. Several days later when one child drew the scene she completely left out her best friend who had been sitting next to the boy who shot himself. Earlier, she and her best friend had been fighting about this boy. Had we not asked the question and not used the information to point out the friend's absence in the drawing, we would have missed the opportunity to help the girl with some very difficult accountability issues.

❍ What was the worst moment for you?
❍ Where in your body did you feel the most hurt?

Very often the child's worst moment is not at all what we would have perceived it to be. For one child it might be the waiting, for another the unending phone calls, and for others the funeral. For some it might be the silence or a father's tears. A child's response to the "worst moment" often identifies a real sensitivity that is not observable until you ask the question.

As for where in the body they felt the most hurt, some may say their heart, others their stomach or head, and others will say "nowhere". When you ask children to describe the feeling, even the feeling of "nowhere" some children will become animated. For example Tommy in Chapter Two described the hurt as looking like "melted pizza," like someone "...ripping your guts out",which he then drew. It is a question that helps children further elaborate their reactions. This in turn helps them to release unwanted feelings and helps you better understand the severity of their reactions.

❍ What made you the most afraid then?
❍ scares you about it now?
❍ What else scares you the most now?
❍ What do you do when you get scared?

These questions can reveal the severity of their fear, their attempts to cope with their terror, both appropriately and inappropriately. It can reveal both realistic and unfounded present dangers and stresses in their lives. Children will often fear that the killer will break out of jail and come after them or that their abusive father will be released from jail and kidnap them or hurt their mother. Others will refer to aspects of the incident and similar aspects occurring in the present such as fire crackers sounding like gun shots, or when alone now, reminding them of being left alone all day and all night by a parent in the past.

Of course, some children will deny fear and others have lost the fear instinct. Children have told us, "nothing scares me anymore." Their parents validate this as well as their own fear that the child no longer fears what they need to fear. This numbed or diminished instinctive fear response places the child at risk and is one of the most difficult reactions to overcome.

- ❍ What was the first thing you thought?
- ❍ What did you do?
- ❍ Is there anything you wish you could have said or done?
- ❍ I'll bet you wish that you________________________

These questions address the issues of accountability and personal guilt "It was my fault" and survivor guilt, "It should have been me." The need to address accountability is critical.

- ❍ What would you like to see happen to this person?
- ❍ What scares you about this person (the perpetrator)?
- ❍ What makes you mad now?
- ❍ What do you do when you get mad now?

In incidents where another individual causes the trauma, revenge is generally present. It is a response that children often hide. They need to know the reaction is normal but not one they can act on. How the children are currently managing their anger is critical. Trauma can heighten aggressiveness, assaultive behaviors, and loss of control over anger. The traumatized child can become physically harmful, very destructive toward others or toward self.

One child indicated that now when he gets mad he hops on his bike and takes off down the middle of the street. This places him in harm's way and indicates a loss of control over his anger. This must become a primary focus of intervention. Some children express the desire to get a gun and "blow away" whoever killed their brother, sister, parent, friend. If a gun is available, the likelihood that they would use it when they get angry with someone else is great.

Asking the child to draw what they would like to see happen to the person who caused their trauma can bring a good deal to the surface and provide an opportunity to release the intensity of these feelings. This allows the child to move beyond their rage and provides a vehicle for them to give you a better understanding of the intensity of their anger, denial of it, fear of it.

❍ Can you imagine what else could have happened?

This question affords the child an opportunity to release additional grief they may be feeling. It also presents the opportunity to order events in a way that lets the child feel in control, to counteract their sense of helplessness. It provides an opportunity for them to draw or play this out with you. By focusing on this "wished for" outcome children can release additional feelings and allows them to return to more difficult aspects of the experience, especially those related to the victim's body if there was a death, mutilation, or severe injury.

❍ Can you draw me a picture of what (person's name) looked like dead (injured)?

This question frequently presents more anxiety for the "helper" than the child. It is also a question that brings about visual and verbal descriptions by the child that can be horrifying for the listener as well. Tommy's picture in Chapter One of his dead sister or James' picture of his mother are difficult to look at as an adult. But, we must realize these images that innocent, vulnerable children carry with them are representations of their unsafe, terror filled world.

This particular area is also the one the children later point to as the most helpful. Most people in their lives have avoided this part of the event and have left the child to deal with it on their own. When someone finally gives them the opportunity to share it they often are eager to do so despite the emotional difficulty involved. It is not unusual for children following this task to let out a big yawn or sigh and somewhat collapse in their chair feeling exhausted and relieved. In all three interviews with Elizabeth, Tommy and Mary the drawing of their murdered sister's body became a pivotal point in their finding some relief. Don't avoid this part of the consultation. The child needs the opportunity to share their terror with someone.

❍ Tell me about your dreams.

Children may no longer dream of the actual incident but they may still have traumatic dreams. In their dreams the most exposed are in the direct line of being hurt or killed. The least exposed will have dreams in which there is real danger but they are not the direct target. Both forms, however, leave the child anxious and frightened. They need the opportunity to talk about these as well as hear that they are normal reactions and that they are not real even through they seem real. We can of course do work to help them "redo" their dreams in the same way they relate what could have happened differently.

❍ Has anything like this happened before?
❍ you felt things like this before?
❍ When?

This addresses the issue of previous traumas that may be adding to the intensity of their most recent experience. Sometimes children will bring past experiences, reactions, visualizations and memories into their most recent trauma not realizing they are describing a past experience. Sometimes triggered past traumas will emerge as a priority in your consultation. Follow their lead. If past trauma material is surfacing, it is because it needs attending.

- ❍ What do you think will happen to you now?
- ❍ What other things worry you now?
- ❍ What would you like to happen?
- ❍ What do you dream of becoming when you grow up?
- ❍ Is that different than what you dreamed about becoming before the incident?

These questions identify current stressors that will need attending. They help to identify future orientation. Adolescents sometimes detach themselves from a future. Hope is stolen from them. This, of course, can lead to severe depression, suicide, and other self defeating behaviors.

Support

After providing the child with a good deal of support and encouragement for the brave way they faced these terrible memories, ask them "What helped the most?" "What drawing helped the most, meant the most?" This gives you the feedback you need and the opportunity to reinforce that talking does help.

Conclusion

As you can see, these questions are quite specific and help focus you and the child on the central elements of their trauma experience. As the child begins to draw and you become curious about their drawings and the specific aspects of their trauma experience, the questioning will become natural.

We stated earlier that it is important for the child to lead you. Some children will immediately deal with detail and facts while others will tell elaborate stories, use metaphors, or describe fantasies they need to share. At some point, however, you must ask questions specific to their experience. Again, their drawings and stories usually afford a natural opportunity to do so.

NOTE: If a child or adolescent absolutely refuses to draw, don't give up too quickly. If they simply refuse, then use only the questions. This will still provide the trauma focus necessary to bring the help and relief.

More About the Process -- Duration of Interview

The actual length of the consultation varies greatly with each child. Some six and seven year olds have amazed us; they were still going strong after 45-60 minutes. Generally this is because no one had been as specific in their focus nor had given them the opportunity to share their terror.

On the other hand PTSD does not always exist alone. Often it exists with other symptoms that can make it difficult to complete this process in one session. Some children will need two or three sessions to cover all the issues these critical questions address.

Generally the process will take from 60 to 90 minutes.

Return to Drawings

Do not be afraid to go back to the drawings. Ask them if they have any more to tell you about a specific drawing or ask questions that come to you as you review the drawings again. This last minute review often yields critical information that had been too traumatic for the child to address earlier.

The Last Few Minutes

Before ending the interview always focus the child on positive memories and positive aspects of their life. Always give the child your card and phone number in case they want to return. Normalize for them that new reactions can emerge. Give examples and let them know this does not mean they are failures or doing anything wrong. Let them know it takes time and that new or old reactions simply mean it's time to talk again.

About Adolescents

Interviewing adolescents can be more difficult than interviewing children. They often shut down, are tired of talking, afraid they are too old for the feeling they are having, or just plain afraid of losing control over their feelings. You may want first to ask them some of the questions presented earlier. After about 15 - 30 minutes of discussion introduce drawing.

Some adolescents will initially resist drawing. We encourage you to pursue your request. Explain that drawing, even drawing stick figures, helps in recalling parts of the experience they may have forgotten because of how terrifying it was at the time. Use the techniques described at the beginning of the chapter to get them started. Use examples of simplistic drawings by others for encouragement.

Generally they will comply when you stress the importance, show examples and get them started. One method not mentioned earlier is to ask, "If you were to draw something about what happened to you, what would you draw?" Suggest they start with just one aspect, such as the head of a person involved. If they're drawing a room, start by drawing a square and then put in windows, then the door, etc. As they draw, encourage them to describe what/who they are drawing. Once they begin to draw and talk they'll complete the task.

Generally helpers have more anxiety about asking or pursuing drawing with adolescents who initially resist than do the adolescents once they begin.

Adults may also say, "I can't draw. I haven't drawn in years." With encouragement not only do they begin to draw but they surprise themselves with the memories and feelings of their past experience.

Trauma Questions

Have a list of the trauma specific questions with you during the interview. (See Appendix) Before concluding the interview review the list to identify areas you may not have addressed. Remember, this will be stressful for you. Your own emotions will be at play. You can easily lose your focus. You may have only one interview with the child. To give them every opportunity to find some relief, check to be sure you have addressed the different areas.

Recording the Interview

The checklist found in the Appendix identifies those issues you will want to address in your interview summary. Again, we advise the use of this check list. You will find this process will yield a good deal of information that is critical in your assessment, recommendations for future focus and intervention. If you are going to be in the position of consulting or interviewing traumatized children regularly, you'll need a good written summary. Should you meet with them again, this will allow you to avoid confusing one child's reactions with another's.

This process is also a form of debriefing. Just as we use drawing to help the child transfer their stress outside themselves, writing the summary helps you release the intensity of the experience.

In Chapter Four we provide recommendations for parents whom you will want to educate and offer guidance to so they can respond to their child's specific trauma reactions.

CASE ILLUSTRATION: WITNESS TO MURDER OF MOTHER

James' Interview

(This is an abbreviated version. The actual interview lasted close to 90 minutes.)

James, seven years old, was interviewed approximately five years after he witnessed his father kill his mother. He was 17 months old at the time of the killing. While his father was out on bond he kidnapped James. The police found them approximately seven months later after James witnessed his father brutally beat a girlfriend who then turned him over to police. James has been living with his grandparents since he was three years old.

James brought a memory box filled with photos of his mother, stuffed dolls he had at age two and other momentos. Of interest was a clown he pulled out that he said he hated but didn't know why. Later in the interview he drew a picture of his father killing his mother. The father's mouth resembled the clown's mouth. After going through the memory box the consultant asked James to draw a picture he could tell a story about.

FIGURE 1

James (J): (FIGURE 1) This is my cousin. We drove a long way to go see him. It was lots of fun. We had a birthday party. *(His story went on for approximately 10 minutes. It was evident it had nothing to do with his experience. The consultant focused on the trauma).*

Consultant (C): That really sounded like you had a good time. Later we'll have time for other stories, but now could you draw me a picture about your mom's being killed that you could tell me a story about?

J: *(For the next 5 minutes he drew carefully and with intensity and concentration. He said very little until he finished).* (FIGURE 2) This is my father and this is my mother. He shot her. I'm here. I was two years old.

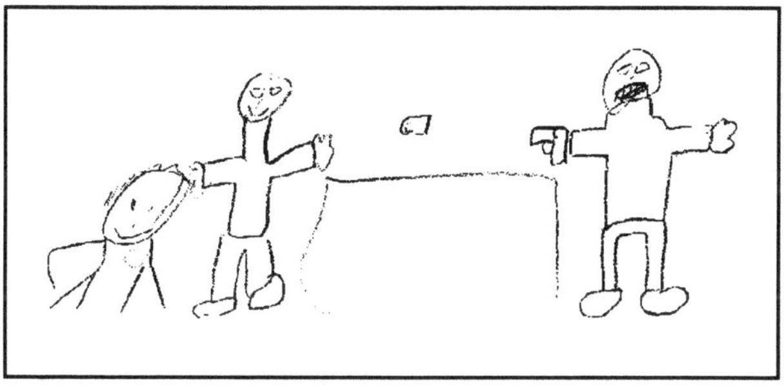

FIGURE 2

C: What was happening at the time?

J: They were fighting and my mom wanted to leave. They were always fighting. That's it.

C: I bet you wish it would have been different.

J: Yes.

C: What do you wish would have been different?

J: I wish my mom didn't go get my car seat.

C: What do you mean?

J: She forgot me when she went to get my car seat and then she came back to get me. That's when my dad shot her.

C: I see. Do you remember anything else about that day?

J: No.

C: Are there any sounds or things that remind you of that day today?

J: Sometimes I hear gunshots in my neighborhood and I get scared.

C: What do you do when you get scared?

J: I stay with my grandma or go to my room.

C: Your father looks very mean.

J: He was always mad.

C: What do you want to happen to your father?

J: That he never gets out of jail.

C: Does anything scare you about him now?

J: That he might get out of jail and come take me again.

C: You mean when he took you from your grandma's after he killed your mother?

J: Yeah.

C: What was the worst part for you?

J: The day he beat his girlfriend real bad . . .I was there but I can't remember him doing it . . .I remember being on the couch.

C: Can you draw me a picture and tell me more?

J: (FIGURE 3) This is the couch and here are the bedrooms and this is the front door. *(He elaborated on the details of the room that actually was the room in which his mother had been killed, not the room where his father had beaten the girlfriend).*

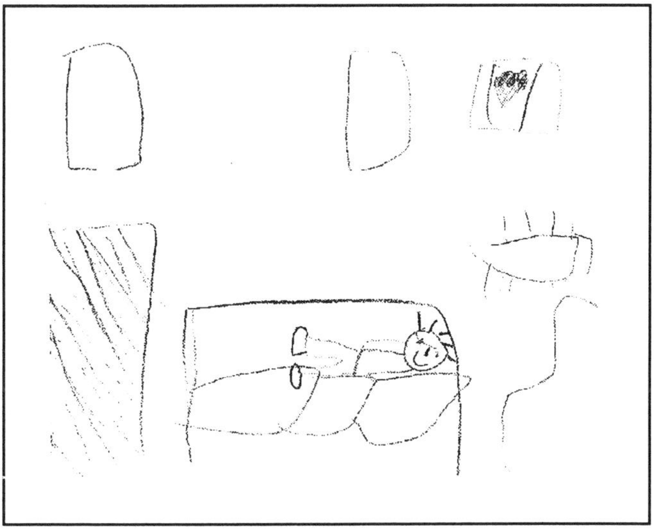

FIGURE 3

C: Where are you in the picture. *(He had not drawn himself).*

J: I'm on the couch *(draws himself)* watching T.V. I was there a very long time like all day and all night. I don't know where my father was. I was scared because he didn't come back.

C: Do you ever feel the same way now?

J: *(He thought a long time.)* Sometimes when my grandma is gone a long time I get scared and just stay in my room. *(He follows her into the bathroom when he's really scared. He still clings to his grandma.)*

C: Do you ever have trouble sleeping? *(Grandmother had stated before the interview that James was sleeping on the floor.)*

J: No.

C: You sleep on the floor. Is there any reason you don't sleep in bed?

J: I just like the floor. It's more comfortable.

C: Do you ever have bad dreams?

J: Sometimes. I don't dream about my mom's dying much anymore . . . Yes, sometimes my dreams scare me . . .One night *(he smiled)* I dreamed I ate too much candy.

C: What scared you about that?

J: I ate so much my whole body exploded. *(C and J laughed then J. added that it "woke me up cause it scared me.")*

C: James, why would your father kill your mother?

J: 'Cause he was always mad and didn't like us.

C: Did you do things to make him mad?

J: No, he was just like that.

C: When you get mad what do you do now?

J: I get mad back . . . Sometimes I fight.

C: Do you do things that might cause you to get hurt, like ride you bicycle down a busy street, or pick on someone bigger than you?

J: Nope.

C: James, I know this may be a little difficult, but could you draw a picture of your mom's body when she was killed that day? *(He immediately reached for the pencil and began drawing. His tongue stuck out of the corner of his mouth as his level of concentration intensified. Without saying a word he drew the entire body.)* (FIGURE 4)

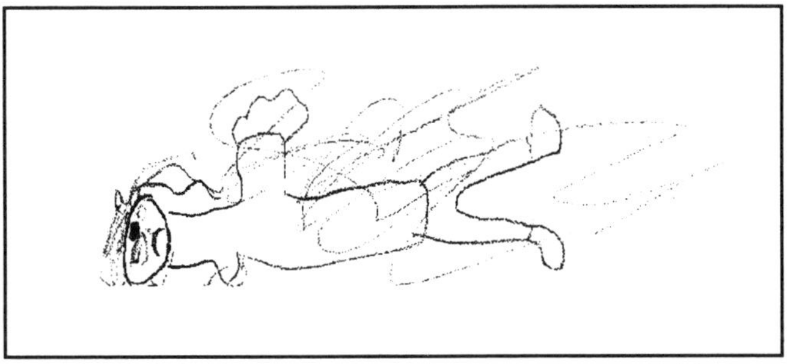

FIGURE 4

C. James,your mother was shot but I can't tell where.

J: In the head. *(He drew a circle in her forehead, blackened it in with his pencil tracing over it multiple times, and then he yawned.)*

C: Was there any blood?

J: *(He took a red pencil and used lines to show blood.)* It was all over her. *(Grandmother reported that there was very little blood. Most of it had pooled under her head.)*

C:	As you look at your mom, do you remember anything else or is there anything else you want to tell me about her?
J:	*(He thought a long time.)* Nope. There's no more.
C:	James, can you point to that part of your body that hurt you the most when your mom was killed?
J:	*(He covered his ears.)*
C:	Do loud noises scare you now.
J:	*(He just shook his head.)*
	We gave James a lot of support and encouragement for working so hard, helping out C. and talking about these difficult memories. Afterward we talked about some positive things about his grandma and then C asked a few more questions.
C:	James, what was it like to talk with me today?
J:	Nobody asks me questions like you about my dad and stuff.
C:	Has anyone asked you to draw things about what happened?
J:	Nope.
C:	What drawing helped the most?
J.	*(He looked for a minute and then pointed to the one of him on the couch.)*

Following the interview, grandmother who had been observing in another room, expressed her amazement at the detail he provided. She said what touched her the most was when he talked about being all alone on the couch and scared. He had never talked about that before. She was unaware that he had been left alone like this. She also indicated amazement about his never hesitating to draw his mother.

A few weeks later the Grandmother reported she and James were going out to get him a bunk bed. James just decided one day that he wanted to sleep in a bed but in one different from the one he had the past several years.

4

TIME WITH PARENTS: THE INTERVIEW

PARENTS WILL...AND YET

Parents will be able to define how their child has changed, yet they will underestimate the influence of the trauma experience on these changes. Parents will see these changes and yet deny them or their severity because to accept them is also to feel fear, fear that perhaps their child is harmed for life.

Parents will see a difference in their child yet not understand or know the differences between grief reactions and trauma reactions.

Parents will know intuitively that they need to do something to help their child yet do nothing because society has conditioned them to believe that it is better to avoid all mention and references to the child's terrifying experience.

If the child is under ten (10) years of age they are also likely to falsely believe that their child was really too young to be severely affected by their trauma and that they will outgrow it.

Parents will be sensitive to the terror their child has experienced yet be impatient with the changes in their child's behavior. They want to believe that the child is choosing or controlling their behavior as opposed to the behavior controlling the child. They cannot accept that the child's overwhelming terror and the need to avoid or control the terror is precipitating and fueling that the child's behavior.

When their child experiences a traumatizing event, parents who themselves have been traumatized will reexperience their own reactions and find it very difficult to take care of themselves and their child. Parents who were not previously traumatized still experience their own terror about the child's emotional well being. That terror can be overwhelming and induce a multitude of difficult reactions that leave an entire family in crisis.

WHAT PARENTS NEED TO KNOW

(See Appendix for form to give parents)

Parents need to know...

That children can be traumatized in the same way as adults

That children experience reactions similar to traumatized adults

That posttraumatic stress creates reactions in addition to and different from grief

That children do not need to be the victim or the witness but only related to a friend or peer of a traumatized adult of child to be traumatized themselves

That violence is not the only kind of incident that can induce trauma in their child

That car accidents, house fires, serious surgical procedures, terminal illness of a loved one, drowning accident, finding a body, divorce, separation from a parent, plane crashes, floods, hurricanes can all induce trauma in a child

That a family trauma such as a murder of a family member can traumatize the entire family

That each member of that family will have his/her own individual reactions

That similar reactions will be intense for some and not for others.
That the longer trauma victims go without trauma specific help the more chronic and severe those reactions can become

That trauma reactions cannot be prevented, but their negative impact on the child's learning, behavior, personality and emotional development can be minimized when help is provided as soon as possible

That children, when given an opportunity, are eager and can face the details of their trauma

That traumatized children generally need to be seen periodically over a period of years, as reactions can take years to emerge

That trauma specific help can help the child find relief from their terror as well as regain a sense of control and power over the "monsters" that their experience induced

That children, when taken for trauma specific help, will be forever grateful to the parent for acknowledging their need to talk with someone who understands what their terror is like

That not every psychiatrist, psychologist, social worker, school counselor or doctor knows what a trauma is or how best to help

That there are questions to ask to determine how helpful a counselor, social worker, etc., might be to their child

That there are very specific ways they can respond to their child's specific reactions

That their traumatized child desperately needs their patience, provision of safety, security and basic nurturing

That they themselves also will need support.

THE PARENT INTERVIEW

(See Appendix for form)

The Parent Interview can take 30 minutes to two hours depending upon their own trauma responses. Our experience has been that combining the parent and the child interview the same day can be taxing on the child who must wait until the parent interview is over. The parent interview is not always necessarily related to the overall outcome of the child interview, but it does support your intervention.

Some staff spent 15-20 minutes with parents to obtain the details of the event. Then they interviewed the child and completed the parent interview another day.

If you must make a choice about what information to obtain, the priority is the incident detail. Before the interview or when arranging for the interview, staff have also gotten much information over the phone, then after the child interview they have completed the process presented here.

1. After your introduction, inform the parents that their child may be experiencing posttraumatic stress because of their exposure to a potentially traumatic incident.

2. Explain that traumatized children can experience some very specific reactions that are normal, but need to be responded to by them. If the incident involved a loss, be certain to add that trauma reactions are different and in addition to grief reactions following a loss.

3. Explain how important it is to determine if their child was traumatized. The terror a child experiences when traumatized, will, if not addressed, likely cause problems with learning, behavior, emotional development and personality.

4. If appropriate, identify normal grief reactions. Then review the Trauma Reactions list in Chapter One and ask which ones their child may have experienced or is experiencing.

5. Ask the parent is they themselves experienced any of these reactions following a traumatic event in their lives.

6. Get as much detail about the specific incident they experienced as well as what their child experienced. Specific detail refers to what they know and what they have heard from others. Details include:

   a) who was there;
   b) what was done;
   c) how long did it go on;
   d) were weapons used;
   e) what was said;
   f) how did it stop;
   g) what happened afterwards;
   h) how were they treated;
   i) what did they feel; and,
   j) all sensory memories or reactions are critical and include sounds, sights, smells.

7. Review with the parents the statements in the handout "WHAT PARENTS NEED TO KNOW".

8. Once the child's experience is detailed, ask parents to attempt to identify changes the child has exhibited since the trauma as well as the child's current status.

9. Inform the parent/guardian that you will share the outcome of the interview with them and make suggestions about how they can help their child. If you have a setting where the parents can observe the interview doing so can be very beneficial. It

increases their sensitivity and sense of urgency to respond differently to their child.

10. When you discuss the outcome of the child interview with the parents, it is important to normalize the reactions you observed and again prepare the parents for additional reactions that may emerge in the future.

    You can suggest that this interview may bring out additional memories or reactions over the next several weeks. Stress that this is not unusual and that it is better these reactions surface now than remain buried. Offer your availability to them by phone or, if needed, by another visit.

11. We believe it is important for parents to leave this difficult session with concrete resources they can call upon as needed. Presentation of materials to them emphasizes their importance in the healing process and your knowledge and credibility as a helper. It can help support further recommendations you may present.

We suggest you present them with the material in the Appendix:

WHAT PARENTS NEED TO KNOW
TRAUMA REACTIONS
HOW PARENTS CAN HELP
WHEN THE FAMILY FACES A TRAUMA

APPENDIX

WHAT PARENTS NEED TO KNOW

PREPARED BY:
THE INSTITUTE FOR TRAUMA AND LOSS IN CHILDREN (TLC)
1994

Parents need to know...

That children can be traumatized in the same way as adults

That children experience reactions similar to traumatized adults

That posttraumatic stress creates reactions in addition to and different from grief

That children do not need to be the victim or the witness but only related to a friend or peer of a traumatized adult of child to be traumatized themselves

That violence is not the only kind of incident that can induce trauma in their child

That car accidents, house fires, serious surgical procedures, terminal illness of a loved one, drowning accident, finding a body, divorce, separation from a parent, plane crashes, floods, hurricanes can all induce trauma in a child

That a family trauma such as a murder of a family member can traumatize the entire family

That each member of that family will have his/her own individual reactions

That similar reactions will be intense for some and not for others

That the longer trauma victims go without trauma specific help the more chronic and severe those reactions can become

That trauma reactions cannot be prevented, but their negative impact on the child's learning, behavior, personality and emotional development can be minimized when help is provided as soon as possible

That children, when given an opportunity, are eager and can face the details of their trauma

That traumatized children generally need to be seen periodically over a period of years, as reactions can take years to emerge

That trauma specific help can help the child find relief from their terror as well as regain a sense of control and power over the "monsters" that their experience induced

That children, when taken for trauma specific help, will be forever grateful to the parent for acknowledging their need to talk with someone who understands what their terror is like

That not every psychiatrist, psychologist, social worker, school counselor or doctor knows what a trauma is or how best to help

That there are questions to ask to determine how helpful a counselor, social worker, etc., might be to their child

That there are very specific ways they can respond to their child's specific reactions

That their traumatized child desperately needs their patience, provision of safety, security and basic nurturing

That they themselves also will need support.

WHEN CHILDREN ARE TRAUMATIZED

PREPARED BY:
THE INSTITUTE FOR TRAUMA AND LOSS IN CHILDREN (TLC)
1994

When a child is terrorized, what happens? A child may

- have trouble sleeping because of nightmares
- be afraid to sleep alone or be left alone even for short periods of time
- be easily startled (terrorized) by sounds, sights, smells similar to those that existed at the time of the event. A car backfiring may sound like the gun shot that killed someone. For one child his dog pouncing down the stairs brought back the sound of his father falling down the stairs and dying
- become hypervigilant, forever watching out for and anticipating that they are about to be or are in danger. (Children who start sleeping on the floor instead of their bed after a trauma do so because they fear the comfort of a bed will let them sleep so hard they won't be able to hear the danger coming)
- become irritable, aggressive, act tough, provoke fights or
- verbalize a desire for revenge
- act as if they are no longer afraid of anything or anyone (and in face of danger not respond appropriately), verbalize that nothing ever scares them anymore

- forget recently acquired skills
- return to behaviors they had previously stopped, i.e., bed wetting, nail biting, or develop disturbing behaviors, i.e., stuttering
- withdraw and want less to do with their friends
- develop headaches, stomach problems, fatigue and other ailment not previously present
- become accident prone, take risks they previously avoided, put themselves in life threatening situations
- develop school behavior problems including a drop in grades and difficulty concentrating
- develop a pessimistic view of the future, lose their resilience to overcome additional difficulties, lose hope, lose their passion to survive, play, enjoy life

PARENTS:
WAYS TO HELP YOUR TRAUMATIZED CHILD/ADOLESCENT

PREPARED BY
THE INSTITUTE FOR TRAUMA AND LOSS IN CHILDREN (TLC)
1994

- Do not be surprised by any significant changes in behavior or personality.
- Be more nurturing and comforting.
- Pay more attention, spend more time.
- Provide consistent care with younger children.
- Let them know where you are going, when you'll be back. If you are gone for several hours, call and let them know you are all right.
- Permit them to talk about it if they want to.
- Encourage them to let you know when they are thinking about it or when new reactions occur.
- Normalize (explain) the reactions they have and are likely to have (See Trauma Reactions List) and, given their experience, how normal these reactions are.
- Provide labels, especially for younger children, for the feelings they are having, i.e., sad, afraid, etc.

- ❍ Inform teachers so they do not misinterpret child's different behavior as something it is not.
- ❍ Be patient with difficulties in concentration, completing school work or other tasks.
- ❍ Limit tasks. Keep them simple.
- ❍ Be patient with regressive behavior such as nail biting, thumb sucking.
- ❍ If their behaviors or changes in personality scare you consult with a trauma specialist, but also reinforce that you understand that these are a result of their experience.
- ❍ Share their concerns for safety, but be realistic.
- ❍ Help them not to generalize.
- ❍ Remind them as needed that "that (incident) was then" and this is now and things have changed.
- ❍ Understand that new physical reactions such as headaches, fatigue, etc., are in response to overwhelming fears and their attempts to avoid them.
- ❍ Help them share their fears and worries.
- ❍ Help them understand the relationship between their anger and their trauma and find safe ways they can discharge their anger, i.e., draw, write, talk about it, exercise, etc.
- ❍ Help them hold onto positive memories of the victim, especially during their most difficult days.

- Do not hurry their reactions along by saying, "It's time to get over it."

- Share your own trauma or frightening experiences. (You survived; they can too is the unspoken message when you share your experiences).

- Help them understand that their now angry, defiant, aggressive behavior, staying away from home or taking unnecessary risk is a way to avoid feeling the pain, the hurt, the terror they experienced. Avoiding, however, will hurt them more.

- Help them talk about what they think could have been done differently.

- Emphasize, if they are feeling shame or guilt, that no one ever taught them to react in such a situation, they did not choose for it to happen and they are not responsible.

- If shame is tied to a physical reaction during the event such as wetting pants, vomiting, crying, etc., assure them that unlike television portrayals, most people faced with terror will lose control over their bodies.

- If they are talking about revenge, ask about their plan and talk about realistic responses. Then provide additional ways to not let revenge take control of their life and to better help them with the pain. Ask for help with this.

- If children express that they are not afraid of anything anymore, "nothing scares me," be more protective of them as they will not act safely in a potentially dangerous situation with others who put them at risk.

WHEN THE FAMILY FACES A TRAUMA

PREPARED BY:
THE INSTITUTE FOR TRAUMA AND LOSS IN CHILDREN (TLC)
1994

It is critical for you as a family to understand that:

All members, regardless of age can be hurting.

Each member may express their reactions differently.

Some reactions, such as not crying or crying "too much," can be easily misinterpreted to mean the person doesn't care or is out of control, when neither may be the case.

Generally one family member tends to take over and is given direct or indirect permission to make major decisions. This produces great resentment in the other members when they realize too late that they wanted to say good-bye by having services in a certain way. Always help the family make joint decisions about the services. One child, for example, remembered how much her sister enjoyed watching the sun come up and asked that her sister be buried facing east.

Be sure you tell the family about the possible reaction they may have in the months to come so should they present themselves, members won't be alarmed or think there is something wrong with them.

Ask relatives and friends for help with basic needs, i.e., bring over a casserole, help with transportation, baby sitting, etc.

Let children and and family members know it is okay to keep mementos for as long as they wish.

Seek help from trauma specialist even if it is just to pick up some reading material.

Expect setbacks. At times emotions will come on like a tidal wave often when you're doing well or finding some enjoyment. These are the feelings that did not get the time or opportunity to be released earlier.

Remember, everybody grieves in their own way and in their own time. For some, two years is normal. Others will begin moving on earlier or later.

For some, cultural customs, additional circumstances or extreme trauma delay the grief process. It may not begin for months or years later when your psyche feels more protected or better able to manage. Frequently trauma victims are unable to respond to their deepest pain until years later. This can happen with any family member.

The responses to be concerned about are those that are obviously destructive such as heavy drinking, not returning to work or the inability after the first few weeks to provide basic care to surviving children or to self. Generally basic care and household routines resume after the first few weeks following a trauma. Periods of crying, depression, etc., are to be expected, but if they prohibit you from being protective of children or self, help is needed.

If any doubt exists as to what is normal or what is a potentially dangerous behavior, contact a trauma specialist. Most hospitals sponsor support groups. Dial the operator and ask for the local crisis center. Talk with them. They have resources to refer you to have your questions answered. You can also call TLC.

Finally, try to prepare your family for the changes that are likely to take place as time goes on. Someone will need to assume the roles of the absent member, the severely injured member, the less functional member. Relationships will change. Life will not be the same. Don't go it alone. Help is available.

TRAUMA QUESTIONS

Prepared by:
The Institute for Trauma and Loss in Children (TLC)
1994

1. What was happening when you found out ?
2. What were you doing? Sounds, sights, smells, etc.
3. Who else was there?
4. What was the first thing you thought? What did you do?
5. What made you most afraid?
6. Sometimes, later, after a long time, other things scare us. What scares you now?
7. Do you have bad dreams? Tell me. How often? Different from before it happened?
8. What was the worst for you?
9. If must have felt really bad. Point to the part of your body that hurt the most.
10. Why do you think this happened?
11. What would make someone do this?
12. What scares you about this person?

13. What would you like to see happen to the person who did this?

14. What do you do now when you get mad?

15. Is there anything you wish you would have said, done?

16. Is there anything you wish you would not have said, done?

17. I'll bet you wish you could have____________________.

18. Can you draw me a picture of what the body looked like?

19. Can you imagine what else could have happened?

20. Has anything like this happened to you before? Since?

21. What do you think will happen now?

22. What other things worry you?

24. What do you dream about doing when you get older?

25. Is that different from what you dreamed about before?

26. How was our talk? What drawing helped you the most?

CHILD INTERVIEW SUMMARY GUIDE

PREPARED BY:
THE INSTITUTE FOR TRAUMA AND LOSS IN CHILDREN (TLC)
1994

The Summary Includes:

1. The story as the child originally tells it
2. The situation as it actually happened
3. The child's emotional reactions to telling what happened
4. Sensory experiences -- sights, sounds, smells
5. Special detailing of any aspect
6. Worst moment
7. Child's visual image of what the saw, e.g., violence, injury, mutilation, behavior never seen before
8. Why child thinks this happened
9. What the child would like to see happen to the person(s) involved
10. What child does when he/she gets angry
11. The child's current concerns as a result of the incident
12. Traumatic dreams -- content

13. Previous traumas
14. What the chid thinks things will be like when he/she is older
15. Current stress
16. What the child feels about talking to you (ends interview status)
17. The questions, statements, reflections you made during interview
18. Recommendations for future focus.
19. How the child's reactions compare with parents' knowledge, observation of child's reactions.
20. Parents response to your meeting and information you provided.

PARENT TRAUMA INTERVIEW FORM

PREPARED BY:
THE INSTITUTE FOR TRAUMA AND LOSS IN CHILDREN (TLC)
1994

When completing the Parent Interview Form, please keep the following in mind:

1. If more than one child in a family is impacted, complete separate questionnaires as each child will have different reactions;

2. One part of this single session goal is to assess PTSD. Another part is to provide the child some relief from their potentially traumatic experience, whether grief, acute stress or PTSD reaction. After the interviews with child and parents you will have good indicators of the actual diagnosis. NOTE: We recommend that you review the DSM-IV for actual diagnostic criteria as time, frequency and number of reactions present determine actual diagnosis for Acute Stress and PTSD.

3. We developed the abbreviated form in response to feedback from over 100 consultants from various agencies. They indicated that the initial Parent Interview was simply too long for the time they generally had for an intake session and that many of the questions were ones they routinely asked at their agencies. All agreed however that obtaining details of the incident and assessing before and after changes significantly influenced their work with the child. It also helped to focus the parent on the seriousness of the child's experience.

   Consultants also agreed that presenting parents with information regarding the trauma reactions children can experience and normalizing these reactions, in fact, encouraged positive parent responsiveness to additional questions about the child's experience and reactions to that traumatic experience.

4. When meeting with parents please keep in mind that without your support and understanding they are likely to minimize the impact of the child's experience. By teaching them about trauma you are in fact giving them hope and supporting the importance of their continued efforts to be a good parent.

Name ____

(Parent(s)/Guardian(s))

Child ____

Age at Incident ______________ Date of Incident ______________

Date of Interview ____________ Age at Interview ______________

1. <u>Incident Details</u>
   Get as much detail about the specific incident the parent may have experienced as well as their child. Specific detail refers to what they know and what they have heard from others. Details include:

   a) who was there;
   b) what was done;
   c) how long did it go on;
   d) were weapons used;
   e) what was said;
   f) how did it stop;
   g) what happened afterwards;
   h) how were they treated afterwards;
   i) what did they feel; and,
   j) all sensory memories or reactions, i.e., sounds, sights, smells.

2. <u>Child's behavior before and after:</u>

   Play

   Before ____

   ____

After ______________________________________

____

School work

Before ______________________________________

____

After ______________________________________

____

School Behavior______________________________________

____

____

____

With Friends/playmates

Before ______________________________________

____

After ______________________________________

____

With Family Members

Before ____

____

After ____

____

Changes in sleeping patterns

Before ____

____

After ____

____

Changes in communicating (talks more, less)

Before ____

____

After ____

____

3. Mood Changes
(Check More, Less, Same,)

	More	Less	Same
Sad	❍	❍	❍
Depressed	❍	❍	❍
Irritable	❍	❍	❍
Afraid	❍	❍	❍
Defiant	❍	❍	❍
Worried	❍	❍	❍
Aggressive	❍	❍	❍
Assaultive (fights)	❍	❍	❍
Serious	❍	❍	❍
More like an adult	❍	❍	❍

4. Does the child engage in behavior(s) once stopped?
(Check)

	Yes	No
Nail Biting	❍	❍
Enuresis (bed wetting)	❍	❍
Clinging (wanting always to be with you)	❍	❍
Afraid to be alone	❍	❍
Others	❍	❍

5. Since the incident the child (Check)

❍ fights more
❍ hurts him/herself
❍ startles easily (jumpy)
❍ avoids reminders of trauma
❍ anticipates danger
❍ is more withdrawn
❍ has more accidents
❍ always seems worried
❍ avoids talking about the trauma

- ❍ continually talks about the trauma
- ❍ remains active (more)
- ❍ tells the story over many times
- ❍ continually reenacts trauma in play

6. What unusual/surprising/frightening behaviors occurred after the incident, i.e.

- ❍ sleeping on floor
- ❍ taking more risks
- ❍ walking/talking in sleep
- ❍ eating changes
- ❍ self care

(in adolescents)

- ❍ alcohol/drug use
- ❍ away from home more
- ❍ others

7. Parents Trauma History and Current Reactions:

____

____

8. Parents major concerns:

____

____

9. Is there anything else you think would be helpful for us to know about you or you or your child?

____

____

REFERENCES

Clark, G., Sack, W.H., Goff, B. (1993) Three forms of stress in Cambodian adolescent refugees. *Journal of Abnormal Psychology.* 21, 65-77.

Eth, S. & Pynoos, R.S. (Eds.). (1985). *Post-traumatic stress disorder in children.* Washington, D.C.: American Psychiatric Press.

Green, B.L., Korol, M., Grace, M.C., Vary, M.G., Leonard, A.C., Gleser, G.C. & Smitson-Cohen, S. (1991). Children and disaster: Age, gender, and parental effects on PTSD symptoms. *Journal of the American Academy of Child and Adolescent Psychiatry*, 30, 945-951.

Jewett, Claudia. (1982). *Helping Children Cope with Separation and Loss.* Massachusetts: Harvard Common Press. 80-81

Kendall-Tackett, K.A., Williams, L. M. & Finkelhor, D. (1993). Impact of sexual abuse on children: A review and synthesis of recent empirical studies. *Psychological Bulletin,* 113, 164-180.

Malchiodi, Cathy A. (1990). *Breaking the silence: Art therapy with children from violent homes.* New York: Brunner/Mazel Publishers.

March, J., Amaya-Jackson, L., Costanzo, P., Terry, R. & The Hamlet Fire Consortium (1993, January). Post-traumatic stress in children and adolescents after an industrial fire. Paper presented at the Lake George Conference on PTSD.

Matsakis, Aphrodite. (1992). *I can't get over it: A handbook for trauma survivors.* Oakland, CA: New Harbinger Publications, Inc.

McFarlane, A.C. (1987). Posttraumatic phenomena in a longitudinal study of children following a natural disaster. *Journal of the American Academy of Child and Adolescent Psychiatry*, 26, 764-769.

McNally, R.J. (1993). Stressors that produce posttraumatic stress disorder in children (1st ed.). In R.T. Davidson & E.B. Foa (Eds.) *Posttraumatic stress disorder: DSM-IV and beyond* (pp. 57-74). Washington: American Psychiatric Press.

Middelton-Moz, Jane. (1989). *Children of trauma: Rediscovering your discarded self.* Deerfield Beach, FL: Health Communications, Inc.

Nader, K., Pynoos, R.S., Fairbanks, L., & Frederick, C.J. (1990). Children's PTSD reactions one year after a sniper attack at their school. *American Journal of Psychiatry,* 147, 1526-1530.

Pynoos, R.S., Frederick, C.J., Nader, K., Arroyo, W., Steinberg, A., Eth, S., Nunez, F., & Fairbanks, L. (1987). Life threat and posttraumatic stress in school-age children. *Archives of General Psychiatry*, 44, 1057-1063.

Pynoos, R.S. & Nader, K. (1989). Children's memory and proximity to violence. *Journal of the American Academy of Child and Adolescent* Psychiatry, 28, 236-241.

Saigh, P.A. (1991). The development of posttraumatic stress disorder following four types of traumatization. *Behaviour Research and Therapy*, 29, 213-216.

Stuber, M.L., Nader, K., Yasuda, P., Pynoos, R.S., & Cohen, S. (1991). Stress responses after pediatric bone marrow transplantation: Preliminary results of a prospective longitudinal study. *Journal of the American Academy of Child and Adolescent Psychiatry,* 30, 952-957.

Terr, L.C. (1991). Childhood traumas: An outline and overview. *American Journal of Psychiatry,* 148, 10-20.

Yule, W., Udwin, O. & Murdoch, K. (1990). The 'Jupiter' Sinking: Affects on children's fears, depression and anxiety. *Journal of Child Psychology and Psychiatry and Allied Disciplines*, 31, 1051-1061